THE STUDENT
ENTREPRENEUR

THE STUDENT
ENTREPRENEUR

Mary Ayisi

authorHOUSE®

AuthorHouse™
1663 Liberty Drive
Bloomington, IN 47403
www.authorhouse.com
Phone: 1-800-839-8640

Published by AuthorHouse   10/05/2012

ISBN: 978-1-4772-3128-9 (sc)
ISBN: 978-1-4772-3129-6 (e)

I dedicate this book to Mrs Augustina Ayisi (my mother), Nick and my three beautiful daughters, Nicole, Kelly-Louise and Mikayla for supporting and encouraging me to write this book. I would not have been able to do it without you. With your prayers, companionship, support and ideas, I was able to complete this book in the shortest possible time.

I also dedicate this book to Modernghana.com which on 6 May 2011 published an article on an award ceremony that took place in February 2012 in Ghana. The article was titled 'Ghanaian Student Entrepreneurs to be honoured on February 24th 2012'. As soon as I read the article I was inspired by the efforts of the TANOE group (The African Network of Entrepreneurs) and the government of Ghana to help give birth to entrepreneurship among students before they graduate. This book is in support of the efforts of the TANOE Group and the government of Ghana.

Thank you so much, and I love you all.

Table of Contents

PREFACE

The aim of this book is to motivate and guide Ghanaian students in their quest to start their own businesses. It is a step-by-step guide for setting up a business, starting from analysis of the business idea, knowing your strengths and weaknesses, understanding opportunities, knowing the kind of product to offer, setting pricing, promoting the business and its products, writing a business plan, registration procedure of the business, and putting ideas into action, including financial reporting. Finally, I have provided about 150 business opportunities.

ACKNOWLEDGEMENT

My heartfelt thanks to the Holy Spirit who gave me the ideas, contacts and inspiration to put this book together. Also to **Dr Shadrach Ofosuware** (Pastor in Charge, Freedom Centre International—FCI) for inspiring me to achieve more.

Special acknowledgement also goes to my mentor and friend, Richard Osei Asibey Bonsu of the British Institute of Technology & E-commerce (Department of MBA), who advised, supported, guided, and checked my work for consistency throughout from beginning to the end.

I also give thanks to Beryl-Ann of Freedom Centre International (FCI UK) for advising and proofreading the manuscript.

INTRODUCTION

I have recently been hit by certain realities in life, especially the mentality of many students toward employment.

I am a professional banker with sixteen years' experience working with some of the UK's leading Investment banks, including Barclays Bank, Lloyds Banking Group, HSBC, Close Property Finance, and others.

With my banking background and the opportunities offered me working in the banking industry, friends and colleagues have sought my advice on various issues, particularly about working in the industry.

What recently hit me was that since 2007 the global job market has been struggling, and there has been a significant drop in recruitment and employment of graduates, making the prospects for those taking their first steps on the career ladder look bleak. Being a fan of entrepreneurship myself, the advice I always give at the end of every conversation with them is to be realistic and set up their own businesses. We, as graduates, have to be creative, think outside the box, and do something for the generations to come. We have to make our own children's future brighter by putting structures in place for them. We have to think of employing people into our businesses rather than looking for jobs—becoming employers rather than employees.

Unlike seeking employment where you would have to compete with a number of people for the same job, entrepreneurship is more a combination of brains and having the guts to step into the unknown. Most universities groom students (including the very brainy ones) for employment rather than to become employers; as such, your competition in the business field is already reduced.

For instance, in Ghana and the rest of the world, fewer large national employers are seeking graduates. However, more small and medium-sized enterprises are using the services of university-career offices to find new employees. The global financial crisis has impacted different employment sectors very differently, with declines in the number of vacancies being advertised by firms in banking, finance, law, and construction and increases among public sector, social care, education, and engineering employers.

When I read the article on Modernghana.com on the student entrepreneurs being honoured, I thought about putting something together to help motivate and guide people in their quest to start their own businesses.

I believe that as a nation if we are able to help individuals to own their businesses, it will encourage and help generations to come. Our children will no longer look to be employed after their education but will have the mindset of entrepreneurship; and since small and medium scale enterprises are the backbone of every nation, Ghana's dream of attaining a middle incomes status by 2015 and beyond will be achieved and our Millennium Development Goals will be reached.

Therefore, any people with an objective, vision, talent, ideas, and the drive to start a new business and who are able to research their competition, potential customers, and their intended business in order to know their strength, weaknesses, and opportunities in the market is in a good position. If also they've developed a clear business plan and are able to put ideas into action, success is certain.

REFLECTION

Richard Lowden, the founder of Eurodrive Car Rental, once said that every time something happens to him, whether positive or negative, he asks himself where the opportunity might be. Let us take for example when people lose their jobs. Their immediate feeling is fear, but little do they think that it could be an opportunity for them to analyze their situation. Chasing after employment may not be for them, but they will need to do a self-analysis to realize that and their potential. Irrespective of their lifestyles and busy schedules, some people are able to take time out and take stock of their lives—where they're at and where they're going. Unfortunately, there are some who are unable to do so, and for such people redundancy could be the best thing that could happen to them as it will force them to take stock.

Alex McMillan, who in 1990 owned a recruitment business, was requested by his staff to produce a list of questions to ask new candidates. One of the questions was, if they could get any job in the world and put on their CV any necessary qualifications, skills, and experience, what job they would want? They interviewed 1,000 people, and out of these, 912 of them said they would want to run their own businesses. This goes to show how people value building a business, and any government should encourage entrepreneurship to secure the future and build its economy. Unfortunately, a majority of people are fearful of failures and uncertainties in setting up and running a business. That fear of failure and uncertainty will stop them from becoming an incredible success, realizing their full potential, and feeling completely free.

It is also said that most people go along a conveyor belt until they receive their pensions. They work for money, not because they are being greedy but to be financially safe and secure.

This book is not being targeted at people who want to work for money or go on the conveyor belt. It is for those who want to make a real difference to themselves: to create, excel, achieve, grow, learn, develop, produce, win, accumulate wealth, and make a big impact on their economy. If you fall into the latter categories, then please read on.

CHAPTER 1

ENTREPRENEURSHIP DEFINED

An entrepreneur is a person who sets up a business venture using their own ideas. They are responsible for the associated risks that come with the business. An entrepreneur turns economic resources from low productivity into a high productivity with greater yield.

The entrepreneur is responsible for leading the firm and has to demonstrate leadership qualities by choosing competent managerial staff to help run the business.

Entrepreneurs have different motives; one is to make money and create wealth. Some of them are also for innovation, and money will help their ideas become a reality and thereby make more money. For some, it is a combination of both. To be an entrepreneur you should be doing your own thinking and making your own decisions—thus, you have to be a responsible person who trusts in your own judgement.

There are two types of entrepreneurs:

1. A person who identifies commercial opportunities around them by being creative, innovative, and having foresight.

2. A practical person who sees and exploits available opportunities in order to successfully make money.

All the above includes small and medium-scale owners, the self employed, artisans, investors, inventors, authors, songwriters, and software developers.

I am of the belief that there are plenty of people out there with lots of ideas who dream of starting a new business with the potential of Facebook, Wayoosi, UT Bank, Virgin Group, Google, LinkedIn, and eBay, but they are not operating today because they fear not getting it off the ground and failing. The saddest thing is that most people have an entrepreneurial talent but are not using it and will never use it. These people can be millionaires before reaching the age of 30. I write this book for all those potential entrepreneurs out there: those with the talent, ideas, and drive and those who are already in business but need to expand or venture into a different field of business on the road to being financially free. This book will release their talent and take them forward in their journey to establishing and growing their business.

CHAPTER 2

GETTING YOURSELF
A VISION

As an aspiring entrepreneur, you have to be clear about what you are trying to achieve and where you see yourself in a year, two years, three years, or even five or ten years' time, because if you don't know where you are going, the chances are that you might never get there.

Case Study: Gloria wanted to set up an off-licence business and indulge her passion for wine. After reviewing the numbers, it became clear that one off-licence was not enough to pay the bills, and she realized that she would be spending every hour of every day working on her business, meaning that she would have less time for her family and friends.

So, Gloria went back to the drawing board and came up with a plan to open three off-licences within the next three to five years, each with its own manager. This clear vision gave Gloria the motivation she needed and also meant that she could fit her working hours around her family. Finally, it became possible for her to put her plans into action in order to make her idea fly.

Exercise:

Analyze your situation now and write down your vision for the next one, three, five, and even ten years. This is very tricky but vital in your quest to unlock your financial freedom. It will also help you to cover things relating to finances, work, family, leisure, health, and wellbeing.

Please complete this box:

	WHERE AM I NOW	WHERE DO I WANT TO BE	HOW WILL I GET THERE
FINANCE			
WORK			
FAMILY			
LEISURE			
HEALTH/ WELLBEING			

In order to get the ball rolling, write down three things you are going to do in order to get there.

Research has confirmed that people with a clear plan to put into action are more likely to be successful as well as being better off financially than those who don't.

CHAPTER 3

IS MY BUSINESS IDEA
UP TO IT?

All businesses need to know key information about their customers and competitors and answer questions about them. When you are able to answer these questions, you will definitely be assured that your business idea is going to work. If you cannot as yet answer these questions, don't worry as there are ways of finding out the answers.

Case Study: Angela enjoys working with children. One day her best friend advised her to use her talent and abilities to set up her own crèche. Angela undertook a careful research in the area in which she wanted to set up the business. She spoke to local mothers in the catchment area to see how many people would need her services and how many similar services were provided in the area. Her research unearthed that the nearest competitor was over eleven miles away, which meant that if she was able to start her crèche, it would be more convenient for the local mothers to use her services than to travel further afield. Angela also undertook research on the internet to have a rough idea as to the hourly rate charged by her competitors and how much the parents would be comfortable paying. For her, having enough information about her competitors and their pricing gave her the assurance and confidence that she could start her business straight away.

Exercise: Please write down the following:

1. What are you offering? Which customers' needs are your products and/or services satisfying?

2. Do you know your customers? If so, who are they and what do you know about them? Knowing these details will help you to effectively target them with your products and services.

3. How big is the market you want to attract? Realistically, how many of these customers are you likely to attract?

4. With all the products and services available from your competitors, why should customers buy your products? How are they going to buy and when would they buy the products?

5. Regarding pricing, how much do your competitors charge for the same product? How much are you going to charge for yours and

how much are customers willing to pay? This information will determine how much you can charge.

6. What is the demand for your products? Are your prospective customers willing to buy your products? Is demand for your products likely to change and, if it does, what would it mean for your business?

7. Think about your competitors. Who are they? Sometimes it is not obvious to establish who your competitors are, so you need to think widely here.

8. Where are your competitors located? What information do you hold on them?

9. Are your competitors' customers happy with their products and services?

10. Why are your products and services better than your competitors? You cannot expect your customers to understand this if you the provider do not know the answer to this.

11. Know your unique selling point, commonly known as your USP. All successful businesses live and breathe their customers. They know

who their customers are, why and how they buy their products, what is important to their customers, and what price they can afford. So, these businesses use this information to their advantage and to make sure that they are clear with their unique selling point.

Let us say you are in a lift with a customer going one floor up, and you only have fifty seconds to sell your products to this prospective customer. How are you going to convince this customer in the shortest possible time? This is called the "elevator pitch". In a nutshell, why should the customer buy from you and not your competitor?

STRATEGIC ANALYSIS

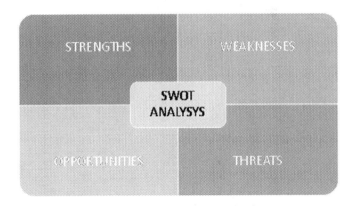

SWOT ANALYSIS

CHAPTER 4

SWOT ANALYSIS

In order to help you unleash your potentials, you have to do a SWOT analysis.

A SWOT analysis is a strategic planning system used in evaluating the Strengths, Weaknesses, Opportunities and Threats associated with the project or the business venture. A SWOT analysis specifies the objective of the project or the business venture. It identifies the internal and external factors that are advantageous or disadvantageous to the business in achieving the objective.

A SWOT analysis must first start with defining a desired end, state, or objective. A SWOT analysis may be incorporated into the strategic planning model. Strategic Planning has been the subject of much research.

Your strengths are the characteristics of the business or team that give it an advantage over others in the industry, and your weaknesses are characteristics that place the firm at a disadvantage relative to others.

Your opportunities are the external chances to make greater sales or profits in the environment, and the threats are also external elements in the environment that could cause trouble for the business.

Identification of SWOTs is essential because subsequent steps in the process of planning for achievement of the selected objective may be derived from the SWOTs.

First, the decision makers have to determine whether the objective is attainable, given the SWOTs. If the objective is *not* attainable, a different objective must be selected and the process repeated.

For a start, you have to analyze how well you know yourself. The purpose of this is to understand where your strength and weaknesses might be, plus what you enjoy doing best as well as what you will rather not do until later. Being honest with yourself now will save you a lot of pain, money, and inconveniences later.

Case Study:

Albert decided to set up his own private business as a marketing consultant, but he also knew he was not good with numbers. He realized that before his business could survive, he needed to keep his accounts in order. Having given the matter some thought, he enrolled in a course at his local college to learn basic bookkeeping.

However, as his business expanded, he paid for the services of an accountant. This eventually helped him to be able to keep on top of his expenses and ensure all his suppliers were paid on time as well as keeping his bank manager and the tax man happy.

Exercise: With a pen and a paper, write down your strengths. That is, what you are really good at doing, and how you are going to make the most of it? What are your weaknesses, and how are you going to deal with them? Where could you do with improvement? What are the opportunities available to you, and how would these feature in your business? Also, write down your dislikes and how you are going to cope with the same. And please be really honest with yourself, as running your own business is a big commitment. Many businesses survive their first year but a lot of them do not. In order to avoid this you really need to be honest with yourself as to what exactly that you want to do. Being honest with yourself now will save your business from failing in the future.

Once you have identified your strengths, weaknesses, opportunities, and threats, ask yourself what experiences you have in order to embark on your new business and how you could make the most of this or plug the gaps.

CHAPTER 5

PUTTING IDEAS INTO ACTION

Maybe you are thinking of where to start. Though most people will have a fair idea as to what they want to do, some people will not, probably because they have only just begun to consider entrepreneurship and are thinking of what to do, where to start from, how to get a business plan, and when to start.

To those people who are new to the idea of entrepreneurship, I will start by quoting Benjamin Disraeli, a nineteenth-century British prime minister. He once said that "Man is only great when he acts from passion". This means that you will definitely become successful when you do things you like doing best out of passion. The best way of finding your passion is to explore avenues of creativity that are likely to be the quickest routes to increase your chances of launching a successful business.

So, someone may ask, what are these avenues of creativity?

First, revisit your childhood. Think about what you liked and did best. It is amazing how we become disconnected from the things that brought us joy in childhood. These are the things we should revisit in order to reflect on our current situation. Let's say we loved doing the ironing—this means that in our current adult life we might enjoy having a dry-cleaning business. If you loved cooking, that could help you in starting a restaurant. Perhaps you used to gather other kids around and play-act as if you were teaching; this could mean that you could become a mentor or a teacher by setting up your own private school, after-school club, breakfast-club, and so on. An American architect called Frank Lloyd Wright loved playing with wooden blocks throughout his childhood, and it was of no surprise that he became an architect.

Second, you should make a creativity board. In the middle of the board, write "new business" and create a collage of images, sayings, articles, poems, and other inspirations. When you surround yourself with images of your intention of who you want to become or what you want to create, your awareness and passion will grow and will help you to think big. As your board evolves and becomes more focused, you will begin to recognize what is missing and imagine ways to fill the blanks and realize your vision.

You can also make a list of people who are where you want to be. You do not have to reinvent the wheel. All you have to do is to study the people who have achieved success in the field you are interested in. For example, you want to be in the real-estate market; however, during the current recession, this industry was badly hit and businesses failed. If real estate is really your passion, do not give up but study those in the same industry who made it and copy their strategies.

My next advice is to start doing what you love even without a business plan. I recommend doing what you enjoy best even if you have not yet figured out how to make money from it. Test what it might be like to work in an area you are passionate about, build your business network, and ask for feedback that will help you develop and refine a business plan. Doing it this way will show the value you bring, and testimonials from your clients will help you launch the new business. Most importantly, doing it this way will help you conquer your fear of starting a new venture, and the joy of accomplishing this will further fuel your creativity.

Finally, please take a break from business thinking. Probably you should indulge yourself in some creative writing, poetry, etc. A day's trip to the Accra Arts Centre could give you lots of ideas. All that you have to do on your return is to reflect on what you saw for the ideas to flow.

CHAPTER 6

THE MARKETING MIX

If you do not win customers, your business will not go far, and even when a business is well-established, you have to find ways of keeping your customers. This brings us to our marketing mix.

There are seven elements in the marketing mix:

- ❖ Product
- ❖ Price
- ❖ Place
- ❖ Promotion
- ❖ People
- ❖ Physical Evidence
- ❖ Process

Product: What kind of product am I offering? What are its features? What are the advantages and benefits of the product?

Price: How much will I charge for the products? What structures of charging am I going to adopt, and how much is my competitor charging?

Place: How am I going to reach my target market? Would I be working from home or have premises, and how best can I reach customers and prospective customers?

Promotion: How am I going to promote my business and its products to the target market?

People: Am I going to employ people or work on my own? What sort of people will work in the business, and what are they likely to say about the business?

Physical Evidence: How do I want my business to appear to customers and prospective customers?

Process: What processes should I introduce to meet my business needs and keep customers coming back for more?

OPPORTUNITIES AND WHICH WAY TO GO

CHAPTER 7

AVAILABLE BUSINESS
OPPORTUNITIES

Children and Education:
Special occasion yard signs
Personalized/interactive music and story CDs/CD-ROMs
Inflatable party rentals
Personalized books and novelties
Online maths tutoring and test preparation
Children's safety products and services
Special-occasion lawn signs
Specialties play equipment sales and events
Personalized children's books
Fundraising programs
Children's toys, books, software, and games
Children's gym, art, sports programs, and birthday parties
Daycare monitoring and locating services
Children's movement learning and fitness
Child and pet identification system
Children's music and movement program
Tutoring referral services
Home tutoring service
Personalized children's books
Inflatable amusement rides
Preschool fitness program
Sewing classes for kids and teens
Children's language education
Children's tennis and golf lessons
Science education products and services
Custom movies for birthday parties and events

Maths learning system for children
Playground cleaning service
Children's bibles, historical films
Baby handprint/footprint bronzed keepsakes
Children's theme parties
Children's music education
Games, puzzles, puppets, and entertainment products
Foreign language instruction for children
Inflatable party products
Bicycles for toddlers
Pre and post-natal fitness programs
Children's cooking programs
Science/math learning and entertainment programs

Internet Technology:
Computer products
Electronic and wireless
Internet consultancy
Video games
DVD sales
Website hosting

Finance and Accounting
Accountancy firm
Audit firm
Tax Adviser
Business Formation
Financial consultancy

Food:
Burgers, fries, and malts
Ice cream stores
Restaurant meal-delivery service
Shaved ice and frozen desserts
Food trailers and carts
Gourmet foods and gifts
Tea parties
Bulk candy vending machines
Pizza

Specialty ice cream
Fresh-roasted, cinnamon-glazed nuts
Donuts and fast food
Personalized candy bars, bottled water, mints, and invitations
Beverage machine rentals, sales, and catering
Fruit and vegetable arrangement design classes
Dinner-delivery service
Coffee carts, kiosks, equipment, and consulting
Personalized embossed chocolate
Roasted peanuts

Healthcare:
Home helpers
Rehabilitation
Elderly care services
Doctors' express urgent care
Homecare
Homecare assistance
In-home companions for elderly people
Pharmacy shops
Private clinics
Midwifery

Sports:
Fitness clubs
Youth sports
Sports leagues
Sports camps
Sports clinics
After-school sports programmes and activities
Football, basketball, and cheerleading
Sports photography
Sports magazine and newspaper
Swimming pool with lessons

Fitness and beauty:
Nutritional products
Haircare salon
Children's haircare

Haircare products
Mobile hair salon

Cleaning and maintenance:
Dry cleaning
Home improvements
Carpet cleaning
Lawn mowing
Cleaning company
Coin laundry
Dry cleaners
Environmental waste solution

Education:
After-school educational programs
Private schools
Small Business/business coaching
Employment agency
Printing and visual communications
Learning centres: maths, English, etc.
Plan ahead events/events organiser
Business advisory
Employee education, coaching, assessments, and consulting firms

Home products and services:
Interior, residential, and commercial painting
Dry cleaning
Carpet cleaning
Carpet, janitorial, and disaster restoration
Commercial, residential, and auto locksmith

Retail Business Opportunities
Sports goods
Children's clothing
Children's products
Computer products
Electronic and wireless products
Food and grocery
Hair salon

Home improvement
Mail, shipping, and eBay
Paint and body
Pets supply
Printing
Special food and beverage
Tools and hardware products
Travel services
Vending kiosk
Photo booth
Frozen deserts
Family entertainment and dining
Nutritional products
ATM
Corporate catering and home food delivery from area's favourite restaurants
Gift cards
Sports clips—barbering shop with giant TVs
UPS franchise
Travel business
Healthy food vending
Arts training with kids, allowing them to keep their own for keepsakes

Travel:
Travel services
Cruises (e.g. On Dodi Princess)

WRITING YOUR BUSINESS PLAN

CHAPTER 8

BUSINESS PLAN

A business plan is like an operating tool that will help and guide you to successfully start and run your business. A business plan is designed to help new or existing business owners take an objective look at their businesses, identify areas of strength and weakness, pinpoint needs that otherwise might be overlooked, spot opportunities early, and begin planning how best to achieve their goals.

In order for every business to survive it needs a business plan, which forces you to take an objective, critical, and unemotional look at your business project as a whole. When you do so, you are able to identify your strengths, your weaknesses, spot opportunities and the threats that come with them, and the best way of achieving your goals. You are able to avoid further problems by properly preparing your business plan.

A business plan will help others, such as banks, venture capitals, and business angels to evaluate your venture if you seek help from them. It will act as a complete financing proposal so you might not need to prepare another proposal to these companies.

For financial reasons, most business plans will end up with the banks so it is imperative that you are aware of how the banks view business plans and what questions they ask because they take risk into consideration. Whilst it is their wish that the business survives and makes profit, they also want to ensure that the loan will be repaid. Some of the questions they ask, for example:

What is the nature of the business?

What is the purpose of the loan?

What is the amount of the loan?

Does the business have the ability to repay the loan?

What is the character and management skill of the business owner?

Note that, if your business is a new start-up and seeking finance, you might not have the experience and the track record that the banks are looking for, but a well-organized, insightful business plan must convince a banker or other funder of your ability to understand your market, demonstrate your technical knowledge required in the field, and the company's ability to understand and respond to customer needs. The plan must ultimately show your ability to manage the business so it can be operated in a profitable way and repay the loans.

When writing a business plan, below are some of the most important areas to be covered.

EXECUTIVE SUMMARY

An executive summary is a short document or section of a document, produced for business purposes, that summarizes a longer report or proposal or a group of related reports in such a way that readers can rapidly become acquainted with a large body of material without having to read it all. It will usually contain a brief statement of the problem or proposal covered in the major document, background information, concise analysis, and main conclusions. It is intended as an aid to decision making by managers and has been described as possibly the most important part of a business plan. An executive summary is a summary of the key decision-making points in the business plan. Even though this is the first on the list, it is usually done last.

MISSION STATEMENT

A mission statement is an official statement of the aims and objectives of a business or the organization. A mission statement declares what the business is and what it intend to be. A mission statement clarifies who it serves and expresses what it intends to achieve in the future.

A properly written mission statement accurately describes the business and motivates or reassures the people who contribute to its success. A mission statement helps to clarify the following:

- ❖ The type of business we are in
- ❖ The type of business we intend to be
- ❖ The target market of the business and
- ❖ What inspires us

The characteristics of a mission statement are:

A mission statement is visionary, and a visionary statement helps the people involved to understand what the business is all about and what contribution they can bring to the business in order to achieve that vision.

It should be broad enough to allow the company to meet the needs of their customers without annual revisions of the statement.

It should be realistic, which means it should be practical and workable. An overbearing, unrealistic mission statement will not have great credibility. Instead, the best statements are direct and powerful.

And, finally, it should be motivational. The mission statement should inspire all stakeholders of the business about what the company will do or produce—for example, its customers, employees, partners, and funding agencies.

HISTORY OF YOUR BUSINESS

This will be the history of the business—for example the founding date, major successes, and strategically valuable experiences.

PRODUCTS AND OR SERVICES

Your products and services should be described here in simple terms so that everybody will understand and should include:

- ❖ What makes it different
- ❖ What benefits it offers
- ❖ Why customers would buy it from you instead of your competitors
- ❖ How you plan to develop your products or services

❖ Whether you hold any patents, trademarks, or design registration
❖ The key features and success factors of your industry or sector

Remember that you are the only one who understands your business, its products, and services, and the person reading the plan might not—so it is important to avoid jargon.

MARKET RESEARCH

You should refer to any market research you have carried out already and define your market, your position in the marketplace and who your competitors are going to be. You need to be fully aware of the market you want to operate in and also you should understand important trends and drivers in the marketplace. You should also be able to demonstrate in a growing market that even in fierce competition your business will be able to attract more customers.

Key areas to cover must include:

❖ Your market—its size, historical data about its development, and key current issues
❖ Your target customer base—who they are and how you know they will be interested in your products or services

- ❖ Your competitors—who they are, how they work, and the share of the market they hold
- ❖ The future—anticipated changes in the market and how you expect your business and your competitors to react to them

It is important to know your competitors' strengths and weaknesses as compared to your own, and it is good practice to do a competitor analysis of each one. Remember that the market is not static. Your customers' needs and your competitors can change, so as well as showing the competitor analyses you have undertaken, you should also demonstrate that you have considered and drawn up contingency plans to cover alternative scenarios.

MARKETING PLAN

The objectives of the marketing plan for a new product, which has no existing market, must identify all other substitute products. The plan must explain the name of the substitute, its features, why is it a substitute, and why your proposed product is better than the substitute. Also you need to have the switching costs, why a new product justifies switching, expected adoption dynamics, and the expected role once the market begins to develop.

ORGANISATION AND MANAGEMENT

The management team will include the names of the board members, owners, senior managers, and managing partners.

OPERATIONAL DETAILS

In this section you have to outline your operational capabilities and any improvement plans. You should focus on these areas:

- ❖ Location—Does your business have a property? Do you own the property or rent it? What are the advantages and the disadvantages of the location of the business?
- ❖ Producing your goods and services—Do you have your own facilities for production? Will you need any investments, and who is going to be your supplier?
- ❖ Management information system—This is to do with stock control, quality control, and management accounts.
- ❖ Information technology—Information technology is very important in many businesses. You should indicate your strengths and weaknesses in this section and outline any planned development of your system.

FINANCIAL FORECAST

This is the section in which you translate all you have said in your business plan into numbers. If you will need financial assistance, you have to state how much capital you will need and the security you can provide in order to get the assistance. You will also have to state how you plan to repay any borrowings whilst confirming your sources of revenue and income. At this stage you can also include your personal finances.

Your forecasts should run for the next three or even five years and their level of sophistication should reflect the sophistication of your business. However, the first twelve months' forecasts should have the most details. Include the assumptions behind your projection with your figures, both in terms of costs and revenues, so investors can clearly see the thinking behind the numbers.

Your forecast should include:

- ❖ Sales forecast
- ❖ Cash flow forecast
- ❖ Profit and loss forecast
- ❖ Risk analysis

OBJECTIVES AND ACTION PLAN

Objectives should be SMART. It should be specific, measurable, achievable, realistic and time bound.

* ❖ Specific—for example, you might set an objective of getting 100 new customers.
* ❖ Measurable—whatever your objective, you need to be able to check whether you have reached it or not when you review your plan.
* ❖ Achievable—you must have the resources you need to achieve the objective. The key resources are usually people and money.
* ❖ Realistic—targets should stretch you, not demotivate you because they are unreasonable and seem to be out of reach.
* ❖ Time-bound—you should set a deadline for achieving the objective. For example, you might aim to get 100 new customers within the next twelve months.

REGISTERING YOUR BUSINESS

CHAPTER 9

REGISTERING
THE BUSINESS

The following comes directly from the International Finance Corporation, which is part of the World Bank. It shows you step by step, the procedures you have to go through in order to register a company in Ghana.

http://www.doingbusiness.org/data/exploreeconomies/ghana/starting-a-business/

http://www.doingbusiness.org/~/media/fpdkm/doing%20business/documents/profiles/country/GHA.pdf

PROCEDURE	TIME TO COMPLETE	ASSOCIATED COST
(1) Check for availability of company name and submit company documents to obtain an incorporation certificate The entrepreneur arrives at the customer service office to reserve the company name and submit the company documents for registration. -A search is conducted for the proposed company name and, if it is available, a reservation is made. -The entrepreneur files the proposed company regulations with the Registrar. The regulations must be legibly printed or typewritten (or in a similar form acceptable to the Registrar). After the incorporation documents are assessed, the payment is made in cash or by a bank-certified cheque payable to the Registrar General.	1 DAY	Name search—check the availability of company name is free, check the particulars of an existing company is GHC5 per search; complete set of Incorporation forms—GHC10. In addition, GHC 50 for registration of a limited company +GHC 10 filing fee for Forms 3 and 4 +GHC 2 per certification of regulations (3).

The incorporation documents consist of the following forms:

- Company regulations (four copies).
- Form 3, Statement of shareholding structure (five copies).
- Form 4, Stated capital (two copies).
- Tax identification number form (one copy).

The forms require the following information:

- Name of company.
- Nature of the business that subscribers intend to engage in.
- Full names of subscribers and shareholders, their addresses, percentage shareholdings, occupation, and any directorships in any other company.
- Full names of the first directors of the company. A company must have a minimum of 2 directors and at least one director must be

a resident of Ghana at all times, of sound mind, and of legal age (not younger than 21).

- Full name and address of company secretary and auditors (a letter of consent to act as auditor is attached).
- The number of shares that the company is to be registered with and the stated capital.
- An attestation that the minimum nominal capital complies with the requirement that a company 100% Ghanaian-owned have minimum nominal capital of at least GHC 500. The company regulations may be drawn up by the party proposing to incorporate the company, or the standard format that comes with the incorporation forms may be adopted.
- The tax identification number (certificate) is usually obtained by the Registrar General's Department

on behalf of the incorporated company. Four or five copies of the company regulations and Forms 3 and 4 are required (auditors, banks, solicitors, company secretaries may each require a copy).		
(2) A Commissioner of Oaths authenticates forms required for the certificate to commence business Form 4 must be completed for the issuance of the certificate to commence business, which requires authentication before a Commissioner of Oaths. The Commissioner for Oaths, located in the Registrar General's Department, usually swears the oath within 1 day so that the company can obtain the certificate to commence business.	1 day (simultaneous with previous procedure)	GHC 2

(3)	2 days (simultaneous with previous procedure)	0.5% of the stated capital as commencement tax + GHC 10 (registration fee with IRS)
Obtain from the Registrar-General's Department the certificate to commence business		

After incorporating the company, the founder must complete Forms 3 and 4 within 28 days, indicating, among other information, the names, addresses, businesses, and occupations of the company's secretary and directors; name and address of the company's qualified auditor; the address of its registered office; its register of members; the amount of stated capital; and the number of issued and unissued company shares. Forms 3 and 4 must be signed by all company directors and the secretary. As the company's commencement tax, 0.5% of the stated capital is collected by the Registrar-General's

Department on behalf of the Internal Revenue Service (IRS). The Registrar of Companies now automatically registers new companies with the IRS. For companies engaged in general commercial or industrial activities, the minimum registration fee is GHC 1 and the maximum registration is GHC 10, as calculated on projected turnover. Obtaining a tax clearance certificate—if the company is otherwise entitled to a certificate and has a satisfactory tax position—will cost GHC 2. VAT is charged at 15% including a national health insurance levy (NHIL) of 2.5%.		

| (4) Deposit paid-in capital in an account

The following documents must be presented to deposit paid-in capital in a bank account: copies of company regulations; the certificate of incorporation and the certificate to commence business; and signatures of the authorized company representatives.	1 day	No charge
(5) Apply for business licenses at the Metropolitan Authority

The cost to apply for a business license at the Metropolitan Authority depends on the type of business and the category in which it falls. Documents to be submitted depend on the type of enterprise (for example, restaurants must have permits from the fire department | 7 days | GHC 91.5 (varies, depending on the nature of the business) |

and the Town and Country Planning Authority—and, among other documents, an inspection certificate from the Ghana Tourist Board). Companies fall into five categories: A. GHC 500,000 in turnover: GHC400 B. GHC 210,000–500,000 in turnover: GHC 245. C. GHC 100,000-200,000 in turnover: GHC160. D. GHC 3,000–100,000 in turnover: GHC91, 5. E. GHC 0–300 in turnover: GHC49,5 Fees are subject to charge by the Metropolitan Assembly, according to law.		
(6) Inspection of work premises by the Metropolitan Authority An officer visits the business premises and reports to the Revenue Accountant	1 day (included in previous procedure)	No charge

of the Metropolitan Assembly, who then submits a report to the Revenue Mobilization Subcommittee of the Metropolitan Assembly. The subcommittee meets to deliberate on the report and then recommend to the Executive Committee of the Metropolitan Authority, whether any adjustment is required		
(7) Apply for social security To apply for social security, the company must attach the list of employees, their respective salaries and social security numbers, and the company's certificate of incorporation and certificate to commence business.	1 day (simultaneous with previous procedure)	No charge

http://www.doingbusiness.org/data/exploreeconomies/
ghana/starting-a-business

http://www.irs.gov.gh/pages/sections.
php?siteid=irs&mid=3&sid=1827

For further information and up to date information on company registration and to obtain forms, please contact the Registrar-General at the address below:

The Registrar-General
Registrar-General's Department
P. O. Box 118
Accra, Ghana
Tel: 233-21-662043/664691

http://ghanaregistrargeneral.com/Home.aspx.htm

SUCCESSFUL BUSINESS

CHAPTER 10

SUCCESSFUL

BUSINESSES

This section will give you an understanding of the common pitfalls of running a business. Every year, many new businesses fail, so knowing what might go wrong will give you a greater chance of success.

Case Study:

Nick set up his new business selling sports products, but unfortunately, he did not provide a good cash-flow forecast. Before he knew it, his expenses were increasing whilst he was still struggling to find customers to buy his products. As a result of this his business never got off the ground.

If Nick had produced a proper business plan, he would have known what his initial outlay would have been. This would have helped Nick to put the necessary finances in place to help him whilst he got the business up and running. Whilst Nick's business idea was a good one, he did not plan it properly.

Exercise: Make a list of ten possible reasons your business might fail and what you are going to do to counter it. The first year of business start-up is always the toughest, but in all this the good news is that the vast majority of businesses are still trading after one year. After that, only a few will fail before they reach the three-year mark.

Now let us look at where your business could slip up and how to avoid it.

WHERE YOU COULD FAIL	COMMON MISTAKES	HOW TO AVOID/ REMEDIES
Wrong target market or not finding enough market	- Not doing enough research to locate your customers or wrong location - Not understanding the needs of your customers - Not listening to clients - Not understanding your competitors and who they are	- Understand and do a proper market research - Do proper research questionnaires and surveys - Analyze the results from the questionnaire and do a marketing plan

Getting your numbers wrong	- Underestimating your cost and not having enough capital - Increase in cost - Delinquent customers	- Overestimate your budget - Be prepared to tweak your sales/cash flow in the initial stage - Plan how to deal with delinquent customers
Financials	- Using short-term funds to buy equipment and supplies (e.g. overdraft) - Relying too much on awards and grants - Not clarifying terms of borrowings from friends and family	- Only long-term funds should be used to purchase long-term products like equipment; overdrafts are short-term funds and should not be used on the longer term. - Consider how much you need and where you can get it from.
Legislation	- Not following rules like the health and safety - Not getting in writing all your business agreements, etc.	- You have to seek specialist advice, for instance a lawyer to draw all the business agreements for you e.g., a partnership agreement, etc.
Protecting your idea	- A competitor can duplicate your idea if you do not register your trademark with the authorities	Please always protect your idea by considering the intellectual property rights issues.

Ignoring the tax man	- Missing deadlines for tax filing - Not having enough money aside to settle with the tax man	- Please contact the Inland Revenue to enquire about the legal requirements on taxes. Do not put this aside for later. The economy depends on the taxes you pay, and the survival of your business depends on you paying the taxes.
Internet	- Over designed website, which is not customer friendly - No database back-up - Insufficient security to protect customer data	- Use a tight anti-virus protection to protect your customers' data and make your website user friendly. Make sure that your customers can locate you easily.
Hiring and firing of employees	- Inexperienced candidates/limited skills - No job description - Unclear employment policies	- Use professional employment agencies - Human resources policies changes regularly. Make sure you are up to date with current legislation.
Insurance	- Being underinsured	- Have a contingency plan in place to deal with the 'what if this happens' scenarios.

In order to ensure that your business is a success, write down five things that you need to do. Nobody likes to think about the worst scenario happening, but it will do you good to understand some of the common mistakes now and have plans in place so you can avoid them in order for your business to be a success.

CHAPTER 11

FINANCIAL REPORTING

Every business needs to keep basic books and accounts for their daily operations. Keeping such books will help you in the following ways:

- ❖ Show you where you stand financially
- ❖ Help in making financial decisions
- ❖ Help reduce your tax liabilities or agree the same
- ❖ Control VAT, i.e. collecting and paying out VAT
- ❖ Help in auditing and keeping auditing costs down
- ❖ Help in discussing financial position with others, such as banks

Some of the books you need to keep are:

An accounting book that is used to record basic information about cash received and cash payment is called a Cashbook. The Cashbook keeps records of money coming in and the bills that the business will pay out. It is available in hard copy form and also in different types of money management software.

BANK ACCOUNT

Doing business revolves around money and this money needs to be accountable at every stage of transactions and from the business owner's personal finances. Having a business accounts enables accountability, transparency and credibility at every level in your business dealings with government bodies, auditors and creditors who will also assess your business accurately.

BALANCE SHEET

A balance sheet shows the financial position of a business at month or year end. It includes capital, assets and liabilities. With double entry book-keeping, financial transactions are recorded and these transactions should balance.

Assets are cash, stock, land and buildings, motor vehicles, furnitures and fittings, accounts receivables and others owned by the company. Whereas liabilities are money owed by the business to the bank, suppliers and individuals, your capital is your ownership in the business, stock, investment and retained earnings.

PROFIT AND LOSS ACCOUNT

A profit and loss account keep records of expenditure, costs and income made from sales and shows performance of the business over a period of time. It also records revenue from sales and cost of sales plus overheads and expenses to show whether a profit or loss has been made.

A profit and loss account also shows a summary of invoices that have been raised, or sales income that has been generated including an estimate of work in progress but not yet invoiced. A profit and loss account also includes purchases made from suppliers for goods or raw materials, and an estimate of cost for goods or raw materials used but not yet paid for.

SALES BOOK

A sales book is a book of original entry in which you record details of credit sales made by the business. Totals of sales book show the total credit-sales of goods during the period concerned. Usually, the sales book is totalled every month, but you can do a daily sales record in the sales day book from copies of invoices sent out.

INVOICE

An invoice, also known as a bill, is an itemized list of goods shipped or services rendered, stating quantities, prices, fees, shipping charges, etc. Once you've extended credit to your customers, invoicing them on a regular basis becomes your next most important task when it comes to getting paid for your products and services. When invoicing clients, make sure that there is no error in the client's address or the spelling of their. Spell out the payment terms and clearly define the due date. Invoices should be typed or computer printed. Handwritten invoices are always prone to mistakes, and for clarity's sake, invoices should be written in terms that everyone understands.

For occasional customers, make sure you spell out the payment terms properly. If you do regular business with a customer, keep a statement of account that you send out monthly. A statement of account is simply a recap of all the invoices sent to a customer during a given month. This statement should list each invoice by number, date shipped, and amount due.

Whether you use a computerized or a manual system, be sure to stay organized and know how your system works. In a manual system, many business people lump all the invoices together, then spend time at the end of the month sorting them out. This system presents several problems. If you are a one—or two-person operation, there's a chance of losing an invoice or facing additional end-of-the-month bookkeeping problems that delay your invoicing. Remember that if you don't promptly bill your customers, they have the luxury of using your money interest-free.

PURCHASE ORDER

A commercial document issued by a buyer to a seller indicating types, quantities, and agreed prices for products or services the seller will provide to the buyer is called a purchase order. Sending a purchase order to a supplier constitutes a legal offer to buy products or services. Acceptance of a purchase order by a seller usually forms a one-off contract between the buyer and seller, so no contract exists until the purchase order is accepted.

STOCK-RECORD CARD

A stock record card keeps track of inventory. A good and efficient inventory tracking system provides the business with good quality and timeliness data which is sure to improve operational efficiency and also helps in managing products, items or parts within the business.

BANK RECONCILIATION

A bank-reconciliation statement shows the items making up the difference between the balance per the cash book and the balance on the bank statement.

CHAPTER 12

CONCLUSION

What you have to do now is to find out whether you are happy seeking employment that will take you months if not years to find. And for those already employed, are you happy being an employee making lots of money for other people? If not, are you ready to find out what life could be like if you step into the unknown and launch your own business?

If you can positively answer these questions, you have faith and can take risks then start something new. There are a lot of businesses that will not require a huge start-up capital so your risks of losing money could be minimized.

On the other hand, if you are not yet ready for risk taking and you have no faith in starting a new business full time, then please find or stay in employment. With hard work you will earn a regular salary and gradually operate your own business in your spare time until you have gained enough confidence to take it on full time.

Whatever you want to do in life be bold and take a step forward. If you do things and act like an entrepreneur, people will trust you and would want to do business with you. Please note that nobody is born an entrepreneur, but determination and hard work, plus positive endorsements, will move your ideas forward until people will see you as an entrepreneur. Also note down the following points:

1. Back up your database regularly to guard against losing your data and to protect your investment in your database design. When you have a back up, you can always restore your entire database or selected database objects. If there is too much growth in the number of records in your database, consider archiving the older records.

2. Employ the right people, because if you can trust them, it can free you up to have time for developing the business properly.

3. Get a website. Your website is your presence on the internet so that your customers, potential employees, business partners, and even investors can locate you and easily gather information about you and the products and services you offer.

4. If a customer gives you feedback, put it on your website. Feedback works like magic. It is a direct reflection of the services you offer, and also it will help you to build trust with your customers and potential customers.

5. Your business cards also have to be eye catching so you can attract customers.

All the best and may the Lord bless you in all the work of your hand, which you will do, so that there shall be no room enough to receive it.

FREQUENTLY ASKED QUESTIONS AND ANSWERS

1. What kind of business should I set up?

A. If the idea is yours and you initially want to work on your own, consider setting up as a sole trader.

B. However, if you have somebody else that you want to work with, i.e. sharing liabilities and responsibilities, then consider setting up as a partnership.

C. If you want to start the business with huge capital and run it as a director on a salary basis and especially if you do not want to be personally liable to the activities of the business, then register as a 'Limited Company'.

On reflection on the above, if you are still not sure about which way to go, then see a professional advisor who will discuss which business status will be ideal for you.

Registrar General Department: http://www.rgd.gov.gh/

2. How do I finance the business?

A. If you have spare cash, use it and avoid borrowing in the initial stages. This will confirm to others that you are committed, and they will trust you more. However, make sure you keep some spare cash for emergencies as you will be liable for the company's finances.

B. Please check with the authorities whether there is any grant available to new starters or any ongoing support in the form of training or even publicity. If you are eligible, they will help you.

C. You can also take a business loan, a business overdraft, or even borrow from family and friends. Should you borrow from friends and family, make sure that they are aware of the terms of repayment.

3. Regarding taxes, what do I need to know?

A. Taxes are paid on all types of businesses, be it sole trader, partnership, or a limited company.

B. Please check with the Inland Revenue whether you need to pay taxes on capital gains. This is when you sell any assets of the company for profit.

Internal Revenue Service: http://www.irs.gov.gh/pages/

Ghana VAT Service: http://www.vats.gov.gh/

4. What necessary information do I need to know about employing people?

A. Employing someone should be very thorough. Please write a full job description, interview applicants, gather references, and make sure you choose the right person for the job.

B. You will have to get legal advice on your employment contracts. This will prevent legal and financial loss to your business in future.

C. Management of your staff should be fair. Please set rules for both employees and the employer and some of these are the legal stuff like hours, pay, and leave entitlements.

National Labour Commission: http://www.nlcghana.org/index.php?CatId=8&CategoryId=4&page=1

5. How do I decide and choose a business name?

A business name is the most immediate way of putting across the image you want your business to have, therefore it needs to be memorable and also should work in different contexts, for example on your website, shopfront, and on your stationery.

You must ensure that the name has not already been taken up by one of your competitors. Please check with the Registrar General's Department. You can also check in the Yellow Pages or Google it. Unfortunately, in Ghana, most of the businesses will not have an online presence, so do not always expect to find it on the internet.

It is important that the chosen name does not limit your potential for growth. If the name reflects on a specific product or services, it might make it difficult to expand in the future.

http://www.rgd.gov.gh//en/services/business-names.php

6. Do I need premises or do I work from home and what kind of premises would I need?

A. Starting a business from home has some advantages, such as reduced expenditure. However you should be aware that working from home requires self-discipline. There are also insurance and legal implications.

B. If the option is to rent or buy a property for the business, please consider implications, such as suitability for the type of business. For example, are there enough parking spaces or even a space to store your wares. The most important of all is location. Will your customers and prospective customers be able to reach you with ease?

7. Legislation? What legal issues do I need to know?

A. You have to check that your business is complying with the latest legislation, for example, employment law, contract law, health and safety regulation, and trading standards.

B. All your business agreements have to be in writing. This will prevent misunderstandings in the future. Contracts also help everybody to understand their obligations from the onset.

C. If your business will be offering credit terms, please make sure that the terms and conditions are attached to every sale.

USEFUL CONTACTS

INTERNAL REVENUE SERVICE

Head Office:
Location Off '91 Starlets Road, Near Accra Sports Stadium
Address:—P. O. Box 2202, Accra.
General Telephone Number: 233-(0)30—2 675701-10
Inland Revenue Service: http://www.irs.gov.gh/pages/

GHANA VAT SERVICE—Now GRA

GHANA REVENUE AUTHORITY
TEL: 0302 675701—9, 0302-953407, 0302 686106, 0302-684363
FAX: 0302 681163, 0302 664938
EMAIL: info@gra.gov.gh
WEB: www.gra.gov.gh

REGISTRAR GENERAL DEPARTMENT

Registrar General's Department
P.O. Box 118
Accra
Tel: +233 302 664691-93
Fax: +233 302 662043
Registrar General Department: http://www.rgd.gov.gh/

NATIONAL LABOUR COMMISION

National Labour Commission
Private Mail Bag
Ministries, Accra telephone: 233-(0)30—2-238737
233-(0)30—2-238345   fax: 233-(0)30—2-238738
e-mail: info@nlcghana.org
National Labour Commission: http://www.nlcghana.
org/index.php?CatId=8&CategoryId=4&page=1